Walking with
BEATRIX POTTER

Norman & June Buckley

FRANCES LINCOLN LIMITED
PUBLISHERS

Walking with
BEATRIX POTTER

Norman & June Buckley

Frances Lincoln Ltd
4 Torriano Mews
Torriano Avenue
London NW5 2RZ
www.franceslincoln.com

Walking with Beatrix Potter

Page 1. Beatrix Potter outside Hill Top Farm - Courtesy of the
National Trust.
Page 10/11. Beatrix Potter photographed by her father in 1889, driving
a hired pony carriage - Courtesy of the Victoria & Albert Museum.
Page 13. Beatrix Potter with her pet rabbit - Courtesy of a private collector.
Page 17. Beatrix Potter, Tom Storey and a prize-winning Herdwick ewe -
Courtesy of the Frederick Warne Archive.

First Frances Lincoln edition: 2007

A catalogue record for this book is available from the British Library.

ISBN: 978-0-7112-2723-1

Printed in Italy

9 8 7 6 5 4 3 2

CONTENTS

Beatrix in Hill Top garden, under the old Scots pine near
the small gate which leads on to the road.

INTRODUCTION

For large numbers of visitors to the Lake District, including many from distant parts of the world, there is enormous interest in Beatrix Potter; in her life, in her incredibly popular illustrated books for children, in her botanical expertise and also in her later success as a farmer/conservationist and supporter of the National Trust.

The visitor attractions – her house at Hill Top, Near Sawrey, The Beatrix Potter Gallery, Hawkshead, The World of Beatrix Potter, Bowness and the Armitt Trust, Ambleside – all display different aspects of her work and are excellent and popular focal points for an appreciation of her abilities and achievements.

However, in the Lake District, which became her home for the last thirty years of her life, there is much more to see which can nourish and deepen our understanding of this remarkable woman. Whilst she still lived with her parents there were prolonged Potter family holidays at five different properties in the Lake District, all of which were used by Beatrix as bases for exploration of the countryside.

It has long been a matter of fascination that the backgrounds to the wonderful illustrations in her books are frequently based on real places, a high proportion of them being identifiable within the Lake District.

Following her purchase of Hill Top Farm in 1905, there were further acquisitions of farms, cottages and land over the years, resulting in a great legacy to the National Trust which, after her death in 1943, established that organisation as a major landowner in the Lake District, with a strong mandate from Beatrix to preserve traditional farms and farming practices.

Although country walking in the modern sense, with maps, guide books, rucksack and other equipment would be virtually unknown to Beatrix, there can be no doubt that she walked around the area covered by the routes in this book. Firstly, as a young woman on holiday, collecting fungi and other botanical specimens, absorbing, drawing and painting scenes which might later be used in illustrating the little books and generally rejoicing in the splendour of the countryside. Her Journal for 1882 records a walk from Wray Castle to Hawkshead during which she had to ask the way three times, was stuck in stiles and chased by cows. Secondly, later in life, as a farmer, landowner and conservationist, personally supervising the upkeep of the many properties which she owned or managed, and also the farming practices of her tenants.

Passing by the settings of the stories, following in her footsteps across wide areas of 'Beatrix Potter' countryside, and visiting her farms and other land holdings, form the basis of the present book, organised for this purpose into fifteen predominantly short, easy rambles in Britain's finest walking area. There is no evidence that she ever climbed any of the mountains or hills or, indeed, had any interest in them, other than as a backdrop to the scenes which she illustrated so well. Consequently, the chosen routes include no mountain ascents.

The text setting out the route of each walk is supplemented by a sketch map and relevant Beatrix Potter information, accompanied by photographs and by an illustration from the archives of Beatrix Potter's own publishers.

The introduction to each walk contains summarised information concerning the length of the walk, car parking, refreshments, appropriate map and a general description.

HELEN BEATRIX POTTER
1866–1943

Beatrix Potter was born on 28th July, 1866, at the family home, 2 Bolton Gardens, Kensington, London. Her background was upper middle class, the family wealth resulting largely from the Lancashire cotton industry, most notably a huge calico printing enterprise at Dinting near Glossop, owned by her paternal grandfather, Edmund Potter. Her father, Rupert, Edmund's second son, was expected to follow in his father's footsteps but chose instead to study, and qualified as a barrister. In fact he seldom actually practised, being satisfied with a leisurely life as a man about town in London, spending time at his club and pursuing his interest in art and photography. Beatrix's mother, Helen, also from a wealthy northern background, spent most of her time managing the house (with several servants), visiting and entertaining her friends.

After Beatrix's birth, a nurse was added to the establishment. The nurse, and subsequent governesses, had far more input into her upbringing than her parents although, as a teenager, she did visit exhibitions and

Beatrix, photographed by her father in 1889,
driving a hired pony carriage near Holehird, Windermere.

galleries with her father. Despite occasional visits to cousins and her grandmother, Beatrix had a stultifying existence as a virtually friendless Victorian child, spending long periods confined to the nursery. She did not attend school, the governesses being responsible for her education.

When she was six years old her brother, Bertram, was born, eventually providing companionship and a shared interest in animals, drawing and painting. Their schoolroom contained a menagerie of pets of many different kinds.

Following short holidays in the spring, each summer the family would rent a substantial house for several weeks, in either Scotland or, latterly, the Lake District. For Beatrix this was an escape from the dreariness of Bolton Gardens, literally a breath of fresh air, allowing her to roam in the countryside, absorbed in the wonders of nature, finding animals, plants, fungi and fossils, and sketching and painting. During these holidays the seeds were sown for the writing and illustration of the 'little books' which came a few years later. The genesis of *The Tale of Peter Rabbit* was an illustrated letter sent to Noel Moore, son of her former

Beatrix with her pet rabbit, Benjamin Bouncer, in September 1891.

governess, from the holiday home at Eastwood, Dunkeld in 1893.

Also largely attributable to the family holidays was a keen interest in botany, particularly fungi and the development of spores. She pursued this interest at the Natural History Museum and Kew Gardens, developing her own theories which were advanced for the time. Unsympathetic treatment by the authorities at Kew, coupled with her success as a writer and illustrator brought her studies to a premature conclusion. There is no doubt that she could have become an eminent botanist; fortunately we do have the legacy, largely at the Armitt Collection in Ambleside, of several hundred accurate and exquisite paintings of fungi.

The start of her remarkable writing career was the private publication of *The Tale of Peter Rabbit* in 1901, followed by its commercial publication by Frederick Warne & Co., the following year. This book, followed over a period of eighteen years by twenty-two others, has been in print ever since, has been translated into many languages and has become a perpetual best-seller.

Despite this success, life at Bolton Gardens continued to be unappealing to Beatrix. In 1905, her desire and intention to marry Norman Warne, of her publishing company, was opposed by her parents. Forgetting their family background, and the source of their wealth, they considered him, as 'trade', to be unacceptable. Tragically, Norman Warne died shortly after their engagement.

During a holiday at Lakefield (now Ees Wyke), Near Sawrey, Beatrix developed a great love of that part of the Lake District. So much so that in 1905 she used her income from the little books to purchase Hill Top Farm in the village. Although she continued to live in London, she was able to escape to Hill Top from time to time and began to learn about Lakeland farming from the resident farmer, who was kept on as tenant. An extension to the property was built to house him and his family. During the next few years Beatrix purchased nearby Castle Farm and then Courier Farm, with the clear intention of eventually becoming a farmer.

In 1913, at forty-seven years of age, she married the Hawkshead-based solicitor William Heelis, who had acted for her in property transactions. Again, her parents opposed the marriage; the duty of a Victorian daughter was to look after her parents in old age. The married couple extended Castle Cottage which became home for Beatrix

Castle Cottage, 1912

until her death in 1943. Her life transformation
was now almost complete. Although,
exhorted by her publisher, a few more books
were written and, despite failing eyesight,
there was some drawing and painting, these
efforts were spasmodic and lacked the former
enthusiasm. A deep interest in real animals
had clearly become much more important
than 'paper-book animals'. London-based
Beatrix Potter, writer, artist and botanist, had
been replaced by Sawrey-based Mrs Heelis,
wife and farmer.

Her father died in 1914, but her mother
lived on until 1932, moving briefly to Sawrey
before settling at Lindeth Howe (now a
hotel) in Bowness.

Land and property purchases continued for
the rest of Beatrix's life, the most significant
being Troutbeck Park Farm in 1924 and, in
partnership with the National Trust, the
Monk Coniston estate in 1930. Much as she
enjoyed the challenge of farming, particularly
the breeding of pure Herdwick sheep with
which she competed successfully at
numerous local shows, her underlying
motivation was undoubtedly conservation.
She had a passionate love for the Lake
District as it was, and had been enthralled by

Canon Rawnsley's powerful advocacy in favour of preservation. Long before the enactment of meaningful town and country planning controls and the subsequent creation of National Parks, Rawnsley and a few others had foreseen the dangers of

Beatrix, Tom Storey and a prize-winning Herdwick ewe at a Lake District show

uncontrolled creeping urbanisation and other developments on the fragile landscape, its adverse visual effect and, most of all, its potential for destroying the delicate balance of Lakeland farming and a traditional way of life. The formation of the National Trust in 1895 was an early manifestation of his work. Beatrix was an avid disciple. The only way to protect farms, cottages and land was to buy them and the proceeds from the sales of the books had given her the opportunity. All her purchases were intended to be gifted to the National Trust, the great majority after her death. Although she was often in dispute with the Trust's Lake District agent, she never lost faith with the organisation as a whole. Not only did the Trust inherit the actual farms and land, but also her ethos of management, which went right down to the smallest details such as the choice of materials in building and repair works. As the Trust has continued to manage all its farms, not just those inherited from Beatrix, in the same way, it is not fanciful to claim that the Lake District farming landscape that we see and love today is truly a 'Beatrix Potter' countryside.

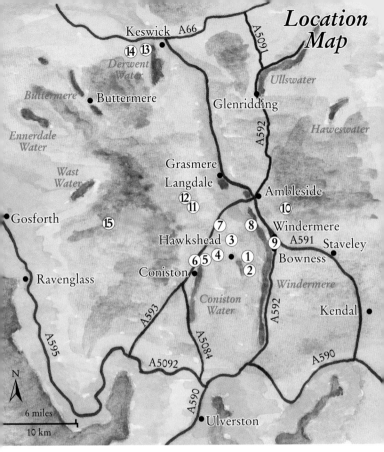

Location Map

Keswick A66

(14) (13)

Derwent Water

Buttermere ● Buttermere

A5091

Ullswater

● Glenridding

A592

Haweswater

Ennerdale Water

Wast Water

● Gosforth

● Grasmere

Langdale

(12)

(11)

(15)

● Ambleside

(10)

Windermere

(7) (8)

Hawkshead (3)

(9) A591

Staveley ●

(6)(5) (4) ● (1)

Bowness

(2)

Coniston ●

Windermere

● Ravenglass

Coniston Water

Kendal ●

A593

A5084

N

A595

A5092

A590

6 miles

10 km

A590

● Ulverston

Each number on the map corresponds to a walk.

Map key

Start Start point

(1) Route numbers

•••• Walk route

•••••• Alternative route

　　 Woodland

1.

BEATRIX POTTER'S HEARTLAND

DISTANCE	5km (3 miles)
DESCRIPTION	A short, gentle, walk generally on good tracks through attractive countryside, with a very small amount of roadside walking. Minimal ascent. One stile.
REFRESHMENTS	Tower Bank Arms/Buckle Yeat tea shop/Sawrey Hotel.
CAR PARKING	Small car park at the Village Institute, Far Sawrey, almost opposite the Sawrey Hotel, grid reference 379954. Box for contributions to Institute funds. Parking probably not available when there is a function at the Institute.
MAP	Ordnance Survey Explorer OL7, The English Lakes, south-eastern area, 1:25,000.

The Tale of Jemima Puddle-Duck

Moss Eccles Tarn

Sheep near Moss Eccles Tarn

Tower Bank Arms

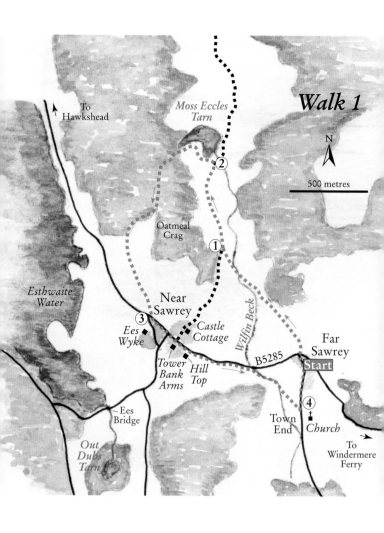

To
Hawkshead

*Moss Eccles
Tarn*

Walk 1

N

500 metres

②

Oatmeal
Crag

①

*Esthwaite
Water*

Near
Sawrey

③

*Ees
Wyke*

*Castle
Cottage*

Wilfin Beck

*Tower
Bank
Arms*

*Hill
Top*

B5285

Far
Sawrey

Start

④

*Ees
Bridge*

Town
End

✝ *Church*

To
Windermere
Ferry

*Out
Dubs
Tarn*

THE WALK

Start Walk down the road, past the Sawrey Hotel, forking right in 100m to follow 'public bridleway to Moss Eccles Tarn and Claiffe Heights'. The surfaced roadway rises, passing the Old Vicarage, with views to the left over Near Sawrey village to the Coniston group of fells. Go through a kissing gate to head for 'Righting', an impressive house ahead. Fork left to leave the drive at a 'Hawkshead' sign. The excellent track crosses Wilfin Beck on a footbridge, rising again to join a similar track from Near Sawrey.

(1) Go straight on, past a 'bridleway Claiffe Heights' sign, rising again.[1] After a gate there is an area of great rocky slabs before the delightful Moss Eccles Tarn is reached, with tempting picnic spots by the shore.[2]

(2) Return down the track for about 100m. Before the gate, fork right up the grass slope, passing close to the rocks on the right. In a short distance go through a gate, reaching a permissive path, which soon becomes a boardwalk over muddy ground. The path winds attractively along the southern shore of the tarn before

1. The high ground to the left is Oatmeal Crag, where Beatrix loved to sit during the 1896 family holiday at Lakefield. In her Journal she has recorded her delight in imagining that a myriad of fairy fungi are singing, bobbing and dancing in the grass, laughing and clapping their hands.

2. The tarn was owned by Beatrix Potter; she kept a rowing boat here which was used by her husband William for fishing. The boat is now in the Windermere Steamboat Museum.

reaching a (locked) gate and a stile. Go straight ahead across a rising meadow, passing two posts with waymarks. After the second post, continue along a distinct broad track, soon descending, with fine views over Esthwaite Water.[3] Pass the entrance to Broad Howe before joining a fully surfaced little road, descending to a small car park and children's play area.

(3)   Turn left along the main road, passing through the centre of Near Sawrey village, with Buckle Yeat, Meadowcroft, the Tower Bank Arms and the entrance to Hill Top.[4] A short distance after the Hill Top entrance take the roadside footpath on the right. On reaching a junction of paths, do not cross the stream; go through a kissing gate on the right, to follow a path beside the stream (Wilfin Beck). Cross the stream on a farm bridge and continue across a meadow, heading for Sawrey church.

(4)   Go through a gate to join a surfaced road at Town End hamlet, turning left to walk past a farm to Far Sawrey. Fork right, uphill, to reach the main road opposite the Sawrey Hotel. Turn right to return to the car park.

3. From the time of her first family holiday visit to Lakefield (now Ees Wyke) in 1896, Beatrix loved the views over this lake. It is probable that her character Jeremy Fisher lived here.

4. In 1905 Beatrix purchased Hill Top Farm, the first of what became many farms in her ownership. Until 1913 her home remained in London, but she 'escaped' to Hill Top whenever possible. The building was extended to accommodate the farm manager and his family (dated stone). Near Sawrey village became the heart of 'Beatrix Potter's Lakeland'. In 1913 she bought Castle Farm, on the far side of Post Office meadow, and also married her local solicitor, William Heelis. They extended Castle Cottage which then became Beatrix's

home for the rest of her life. Settings for illustrations in the 'little books' are abundant; *The Tale of the Two Bad Mice* – possibly some contents of the dolls' house inside Hill Top; *The Tale of the Pie and the Patty-Pan* – Duchess in the garden of Buckle Yeat and the view of Hill Top from the adjacent meadow; *The Tale of Tom Kitten* – scenes inside Hill Top and along Stoney Lane; *The Tale of Jemima Puddle-duck* – the Tower Bank Arms; *The Tale of* *Samuel Whiskers* – scenes inside Hill Top; *The Tale of Ginger and Pickles* – the house 'Meadowcroft' was the shop in this story. After the death of her father, Beatrix moved her widowed mother to Beech House, Near Sawrey for some months, prior to her settlement at Lindeth Howe for the rest of her life. Her coachman, Beckett, and his family occupied Buckle Yeat during her stay in Near Sawrey.

Stoney Lane

2.
NEAR SAWREY
AND CASTLE WOODS

DISTANCE	3½ km (2¼ miles)
DESCRIPTION	A pleasant, easy walk combining a very minor road with an excellent track through the woodland above Beatrix Potter's farms in Near Sawrey. Views of Esthwaite Water and the Coniston group of fells.
REFRESHMENTS	Tower Bank Arms/Buckle Yeat tea shop.
CAR PARKING	National Trust car park in Near Sawrey, grid reference 370957. This area was Beatrix Potter's orchard. The former Courier Farm is behind the car park.
MAP	Ordnance Survey Explorer OL7, The English Lakes, south-eastern area, 1:25,000.

The Tale of Mr. Jeremy Fisher

Signpost close to Near Sawrey

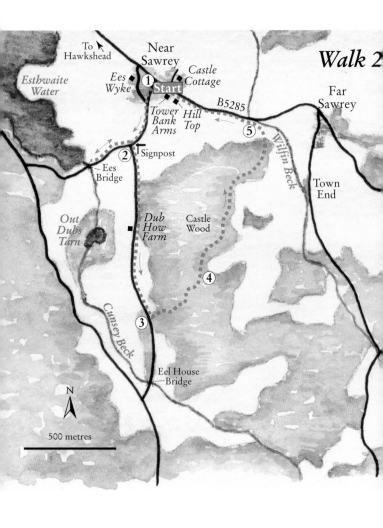

To Hawkshead

Near Sawrey

Castle Cottage

Esthwaite Water

Ees Wyke

① **Start**

Walk 2

Far Sawrey

B5285

Tower Bank Arms

Hill Top

⑤

Wilfin Beck

② Signpost

Ees Bridge

Town End

Out Dubs Tarn

Dub How Farm

Castle Wood

④

Cunsey Beck

③

N

Eel House Bridge

500 metres

THE WALK

Start From the car park turn left along the road, towards Hawkshead.

① In 40m turn left at a road junction to follow the minor road signposted 'Lakeside', descending gently. At a junction in 120m go straight ahead.

② At the next junction (See photograph on p30) the route continues to the left. This junction features in *The Tale of Pigling Bland*.[1] To visit the shore of Esthwaite Water, much admired by Beatrix and probable home of Jeremy Fisher in the 'Tale' of the same name, detour to the right from the junction for 300m or so. The solid stone Ees Bridge crosses Cunsey Beck, the outlet stream from the lake.[2] The shore of the lake can be accessed from beside the bridge, with lovely views along the lake to the mountains. If the detour has been made, return to the junction and turn right to continue along a minor

1. Across the fields to the right is the large house Ees Wyke, formerly named Lakefield. This was a holiday home for the Potter family in 1896, when Beatrix first fell in love with the surrounding area. Her Journal has an entry for 25th July, 1896 'played much with Peter Rabbit' (one of her pets at the time). The all-time best-seller, *The Tale of Peter Rabbit*, was published five years later.

2. Beatrix provided stone from one of her quarries for the repair of this bridge after she had purchased Hill Top and other farms at Near Sawrey.

Esthwaite Water

road, soon passing Dub How Farm.
Below, to the right is the tiny, reed-
fringed, Out Dub Tarn.

③ Approximately 500m. beyond
the farm, turn left at a 'public
footpath' signpost and go through a
farm gate to take a broad track into
woodland. In 50m fork right along a
narrow track, rising more steeply. The
woodland is attractively diverse, with
plenty of silver birch. Cross a muddy
area on a boardwalk and continue
towards a kissing gate at the far end
of the wood.

3. Both of these paths would have been well known to Beatrix, as they adjoin her Sawrey farming land.

④ A few metres before the kissing gate, turn left along a permissive footpath with explanatory sign. A clear path traverses Castle Wood and Hawkshead Flat Wood.[3] White waymarks are plentiful and the route is easy to follow. The buildings of Far Sawrey village can occasionally be seen through the trees on the right. After a short, sharp ascent, descend to a gate and continue along a path between fences to join the public footpath which connects Near and Far Sawrey villages.

⑤ Turn left to pass through three gates and walk, beside Wilfin Beck initially, towards Near Sawrey. At the top of a gentle rise the village comes into view, beautifully set against the mountains. Go through a gate to join the public road, pass the Hill Top entrance and the Tower Bank Arms before returning to the car park.[4] Children might like to visit a small playground (with car park) about 150m further along the Hawkshead road.

4. The numerous Beatrix Potter references in the village are set out in WALK 1.

Gardens at Hill Top Farm

Hill Top, Near Sawrey

Castle Cottage after extension by Betatrix Potter

3.
HAWKSHEAD AND
THE LOANTHWAITE FARMS

DISTANCE	3¾ km (2⅓ miles). Optional extensions include the ascent of Latterbarrow and a ramble through some of the Claiffe woodland adding, for the longer extension, approximately 3½ km. (2¼ miles).
DESCRIPTION	The basic route is a gentle undemanding walk in the farming countryside around Hawkshead, visiting two farms purchased by Beatrix Potter late in life and the hamlet of Colthouse. Latterbarrow is an attractive hill, a good viewpoint that reaches a modest 244m (801ft) above sea level.
REFRESHMENTS	Inns and cafes in Hawkshead.

The Tale of Johnny Town-Mouse

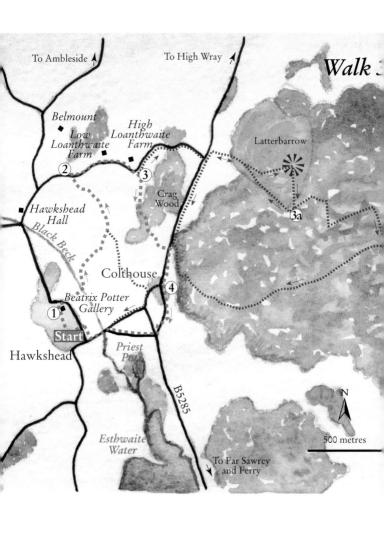

To Ambleside ↑

To High Wray ↑

Walk 3

Belmount ■

Low Loanthwaite Farm ■

High Loanthwaite Farm ■

②

③

Latterbarrow

Crag Wood

■ *Hawkshead Hall*

Black Beck

3a

Colthouse

④

Beatrix Potter Gallery

①

Start

Hawkshead

Priest Pot

B5285

Esthwaite Water

N

500 metres

To Far Sawrey and Ferry ↓

CAR PARKING	Extensive public car park in Hawks head, with public conveniences, grid reference 353980.
MAP	Ordnance Survey Explorer OL7, The English Lakes, south-eastern area, 1:25,000.

THE WALK

1. Hawkshead was well known to Beatrix Potter, as the nearest and most accessible small town to her home in Near Sawrey. In her Journal for 1896, when the family had a long holiday at Lakefield (now Ees Wyke), Sawrey, she mentions attending Hawkshead Show. A visit to the remains of Hawkshead Hall – the 'Courthouse', resulted in a fine watercolour painting and a photograph of Beatrix taken by her father. In *The Tale of Johnny Town-Mouse* there is a picture of a cart in an identifiable Hawkshead scene (See illustration on p39).

2. Beatrix married William Heelis in 1913. The office, owned by the National Trust, houses a great collection of the original illustrations for the little books

Start   From the car park turn towards the town centre, facing the Old Grammar School, attended by William Wordsworth. Turn right to walk along Main Street.[1] Pass the Queen's Head Inn and the former office of William Heelis, solicitor.[2]

① Turn right at Red Lion Yard to walk over the old cobbles to a little gate giving access to the by-pass road. Go straight across to follow a 'footpath to Scar House Lane' signpost. Turn right in 40m to pass a dwelling. On the left is a good example of slate-on-edge walling, common around Hawkshead. Cross Black Beck on the footbridge, turn left then

Hawkshead Village and other Potter memorabilia. Changing each year, a proportion of the illustrations are on public view. *The Tale of the Pie and the Patty-Pan* has an illustration with part of what is now the Beatrix Potter Gallery.

3. Straight ahead is an impressive house, Belmount, the home of a friend, later bought by Beatrix.

angle to the right, across a meadow, to a kissing gate. Go through another kissing gate and then through a little gate to join a broader track – Scar House Lane, now usable only by walkers and cyclists. Turn left to follow the attractive lane, lined with bluebells and other flowers in Spring, to its junction with a surfaced public road, Loanthwaite Lane.[3]

(2)   Turn right, uphill, along the very quiet road, soon reaching Low Loanthwaite Farm.[4] Continue for 150m to High Loanthwaite Farm, purchased at the same time as its neighbour. After High Loanthwaite, ignore the first possible right turn, leading back to Scar House Lane.

Slate on edge wall,
Hawkshead

④ Low Loanthwaite
Farm, purchased by
Beatrix in 1936, just
seven years before
her death.

③ Turn right less than 100m after
the farm, through a gate with a
'Colthouse' signpost. The track follows the
bottom edge of a field before reaching
Crag Wood, beautifully natural and
carpeted with bluebells in Spring. At the
far end of the wood go through a waymarked gate. Latterbarrow is in view to the
left. Pass the house 'Croftlands' and cross a
stream before joining the public road. Turn
right along the roadside, with views over
Hawkshead to the Coniston mountains,
soon reaching the hamlet of Colthouse.
For the shortest return to Hawkshead
turn right at the first junction.

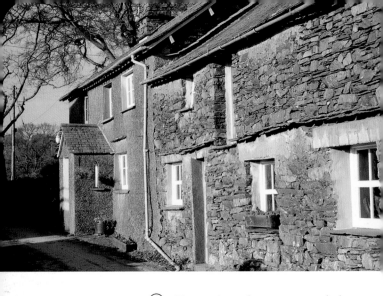

Low Loanthwaite Farm

5. In her Journal Beatrix wrote at some length about attending a meeting here in 1896. Although not a Quaker herself she had an apparent appreciation of Quaker meetings – 'so exactly quaint and fine' in this case.

④ To continue the recommended circuit turn left, following 'Quaker Meeting House 150yds'. Pass the unpretentious meeting house.[5] Pass the extensive Town End Farm, with part used by Hawkshead Brewery, and descend to a road junction. Turn left and join a more important road, turning right to walk by the roadside back to Hawkshead and the car park, crossing Black Beck on the way.

Sheep at High Loanthwaite Farm

For the extension to ascend Latterbarrow, and possibly Claiffe woodland, do not turn right at point 3. Continue along Loanthwaite Lane to a splayed junction with the Colthouse to Wray road. Turn left. In less than 100m turn right at a 'public footpath' signpost, go through a gate and pass a National Trust 'Latterbarrow' sign. Commence the quite steep ascent of the hillside immediately, on a clear track. Keep left at a fork to head directly for the top of the hill. The views over Hawkshead, towards Wetherlam and the Coniston Fells, Crinkle Crags, Bowfell and the Langdale Pikes are superb. There is an engineered section of the path before the summit is reached.

The summit is marked by a well-constructed stone obelisk; the extensive views include Ambleside, the top end of Windermere and a wonderful array of mountains – Helvellyn,

Hawkshead Village

Fairfield, High Street and Seat Sandal
being prominent.

From the obelisk head south along
a good track through the bracken,
descending steadily to join a more
important track beside a gate, point
(3a). Turn right to return to the public
highway, then turn left to walk along
the roadside towards Colthouse,

Beatrix Potter Gallery,
Hawkshead

rejoining the basic route a short
distance before point 4.

For a more extended walk turn left
at point 3a, go over the stile and
follow a clear track through the
woodland. Pass many trees uprooted
by winter storms, soon reaching a gap
in a stone wall. At this point there may
be a notice warning of tree-felling
operations ahead and forbidding
public access. If so, turn round and
proceed to the road, as above.

Otherwise, go through the gap, to a junction in 60m. Turn right, rising gently past the rather desolate felled area. Re-enter living woodland as the track narrows. Reach a stone wall, turning right. In 100m turn left through a gap in the wall. There are arrows on the ground. Descend a steep, awkward bank. The track bears to the left initially, soon reaching the remains of another stone wall, the path now rising. A third stone wall converges from the left as another felled area is passed.

Reach a junction by a gate. There is a three-way signpost. Turn right towards 'bridleway Hawkshead' to follow a broad track, initially between a wall and a fence, soon descending steadily. Pass a tiny tarn on the left, resplendent with rushes and lilies. At a fork bear right to descend to a gate. Rejoin the road close to point 4, turning left to walk to Colthouse.

4.
TARN HOWS AND ROSE CASTLE

DISTANCE 3½ km (2¼ miles).

DESCRIPTION The very popular and beautiful circuit of Lakeland's favourite tarn is an entirely easy ramble with very little ascent and no problems underfoot. It may come as a surprise to realise that the immediate landscape is man-made, the tarn being the result of damming a marshy valley to provide water power for a sawmill. The planting of the oak, rowan, larch and spruce trees has provided a perfect setting for this undoubted jewel. This walk adds a short diversion to the basic circuit, visiting Rose Castle. Despite the name, this is a cottage of modest dimensions, tucked away above the tarn, accessed only by footpaths and a rough, unsurfaced roadway.

The Tale of Jemima Puddle-Duck

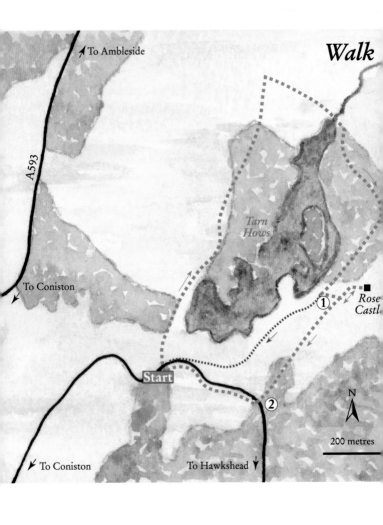

Walk

To Ambleside

A593

To Coniston

Tarn Hows

① Rose Castl

To Coniston

Start

②

To Hawkshead

N

200 metres

REFRESHMENTS	None, but many lovely picnic places around the tarn.
CAR PARKING	National Trust car park (free to members) by the side of the Tarn Hows access road, grid reference 325995. Special car park for the disabled, with its own track and viewpoint, is situated 400m before the main car park. By car the tarn is accessed from the Hawkshead to Coniston road. From Hawkshead turn right at Hawkshead Hill and go straight ahead at two further minor road junctions, following the signpost-ing. From Coniston drive towards Hawkshead Hill, turning left at two junctions. There is only one road giving access to the tarn, which continues as a one way only road to head back towards Coniston.
MAP	Ordnance Survey, Explorer OL7, The English Lakes, south-eastern area, 1:25,000.

Rose Castle

Tarn Hows

THE WALK

1. Beatrix Potter purchased the tarn and surrounding land, in partnership with the National Trust, as part of the Monk Coniston estate in 1930. She did not want to retain ownership of the tarn as it had already become a popular tourist destination. Her primary interest was in farming and conservation, not tourism. As part of the deal with the Trust, however, she retained management of the area for some years.

2. After the Monk Coniston purchase Rose Castle was managed by Beatrix. Following disputes with the Medical Officer of Health and the Sanitary Inspector of the local Council in respect of other properties, Beatrix recorded her relief that this remote property had escaped their attention, as overcrowding was such that there were eight beds in one small room, formerly a servant's bedroom.

Start From the car park, cross the road and follow the broad track down the bank. Continue round the tarn in a clockwise direction. The splendid mountain views include the Langdale Pikes, Fairfield and High Street. With the exception of 1, below, ignore any connecting paths which lead away from the tarn. [1]

① To visit Rose Castle turn left from the main track about three quarters of the way round the tarn, rising to join another broad track which is the access roadway to the cottage. Turn sharp left along this track, reaching Rose Castle in about 200m. [2] Retrace the same route back to the junction and either descend to resume the original circuit OR continue along the upper path to reach the public road through the small car park for the disabled.

② Turn right to walk along the road to the main car park.

5.
FIVE FARMS AND A POT OF TEA

DISTANCE   6 km (3¾ miles)

DESCRIPTION   An attractive circular walk,
                        generally on good tracks, with
                        one gentle but prolonged rise
                        and one section of indistinct
                        footpath. One easy stile. Good
                        views, including Coniston Water.

REFRESHMENTS   Tea room at Yew Tree Farm (or a
                        selection of inns and cafes in
                        Coniston).

CAR PARKING   Pay and Display public car park,
                        with public conveniences, close
                        to the head of Coniston Water,
                        grid reference 316979.

MAP   Ordnance Survey Explorer OL7,
                        The English Lakes, south-eastern
                        area, 1:25,000.

The Tale of Tom Kitten

FIVE FARMS AND A POT OF TEA · 59

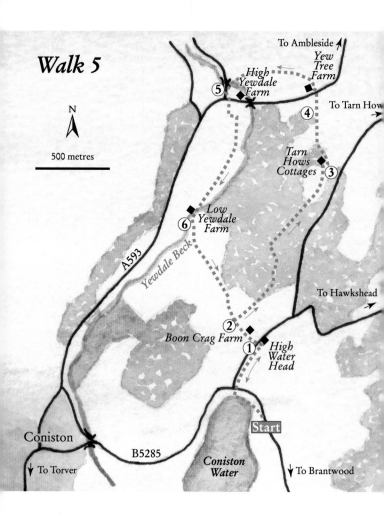

Walk 5

N

500 metres

To Ambleside ↗

Yew Tree Farm

High Yewdale Farm

⑤

To Tarn How

④

Tarn Hows Cottages

③

Low Yewdale Farm

⑥

A593

Yewdale Beck

To Hawkshead ↗

②

Boon Crag Farm

①

High Water Head

Start

Coniston

B5285

↓ To Torver

Coniston Water

↓ To Brantwood

THE WALK

1. This walk is entirely included within the extensive former Monk Coniston estate, purchased by Beatrix Potter in 1930 after lengthy negotiations. Not having sufficient funds to buy the whole estate outright, Beatrix proposed a 50/50 partnership with the National Trust. After a successful fund-raising campaign, the Trust made its contribution and the various properties, which included fourteen farms and Tarn Hows, were duly apportioned. Not having its own agent for the area, the Trust asked Beatrix to manage its properties in conjunction with her own. This situation continued for some years, Beatrix thus becoming manager of a very considerable estate. She later gloated a little that she had benefitted most from the deal. High Waterhead was part of that estate, retained by Beatrix. After her death in 1943, all her farms and land passed to the National Trust, subject only to a life interest for her husband, who died less than two years later.

Start From the car park walk to the nearby road junction. Cross the Coniston to Hawkshead road to a gap in the hedge opposite and turn right along the roadside footpath.

① In about 350m rejoin the road briefly, then turn left by the buildings of High Waterhead Farm in a few metres.[1]

Pass the National Trust woodyard and rise to pass the neat buildings of Boon Crag Farm, another of the farms retained by Beatrix. Continue rising along a broad, stony, track, bearing right at a 'Low Yewdale' signpost. In a further 100m look out for a waymarked farm gate on the right.

② Go through the gate and commence the long, gentle ascent along an evident path across a large field. As height is gained there are views to the Yewdale Fells to the left and back over Coniston Water. The path soon becomes more distinct;

Yew Tree Farm

go through a waymarked gate, continuing to rise. Immediately after passing a clump of mature beeches on the left, the track is indistinct for a short distance. Bear a little to the right and keep a wire fence on the right to rise to a waymarked gate/stile. In a further 100m, at an apparent fork, bear left towards fenced woodland and follow a broad track along the edge of the woodland. Go through another gate, then a farm gate, to reach a surfaced roadway and Tarn Hows Cottages, a neat farmstead, part of the Monk Coniston estate.

Beatrix Potter Tea Room

2. After the purchase of the estate, this farm passed to the National Trust, with Beatrix as manager for some years. In 1933 she encouraged the tenant's wife to open a tea room, providing some of her own furniture to assist. The present tenant's wife has re-opened the tea room, with Beatrix's furniture still in use.

③   Ignore the signpost, going straight ahead between house and barn, crossing the grass to reach a farm gate with National Trust waymark. Turn left, downhill, then left again through a small gate in 30m. The path is indistinct as it bends sharp right to continue the descent of the hillside. Keep close to a wall, then a fence, on the right to reach a waymarked stile. Go over, pass a waymark on a post and continue the descent across grazing land, towards the Coniston to Ambleside road, passing another waymark before reaching the road at a gate almost opposite Yew Tree Farm.[2]

High Yewdale Farm

④ Cross over to the farm entrance, over Yewdale Beck and bear right, through a gate and along an unsurfaced lane, rising gently. Ignore a farm gate, bearing left to a kissing gate in a short distance. Ignore the waymark, turning left immediately after the kissing gate to stay close to a fence, then a wall, on the left, following a good if somewhat cattle-churned track. Pass through four gates before joining a minor road.

⑤ Turn left, cross Yewdale Beck again and continue to the Ambleside to Coniston road, in about 150m. Turn left, reach High Yewdale Farm.[3] Turn right, opposite the farm, through a kissing gate signposted 'public footpath Coniston'. A level grass track now heads towards Coniston, with a good example of a slate slab wall on the right. There are several gates and a plank bridge before the attractive buildings of Low Yewdale Farm,

3. Another of the Monk Coniston estate farms, retained by Beatrix. In 2005 the future of this farm became controversial when, on the retirement of the tenant farmer, The National Trust decided not to re-let the farm but to apportion the land and the landlord's stock between three adjacent Trust-owned farms, the farmhouse to be let for residential use only.

Boon Crag Farm

yet another of Beatrix's Monk Coniston purchases are reached. Go left in front of the barn to a signpost in a few metres. Turn left along a broad track following ⑥ 'Boon Crag and Tarn Hows', cross Yewdale Beck yet again to another signpost 'Boon Crag, Coniston and Cumbria Way' soon rising gently. Pass another signpost before descending to rejoin the outward route at point 2 and return to the car park.

6.
CONISTON

DISTANCE   4 km (2½ miles)

DESCRIPTION   This circuit, based on Coniston,
                  is one of the shorter walks in the
                  book, using part of the Cumbria
                  Way designated footpath
                  through Beatrix Potter farming
                  country. The ascent, most of
                  which occurs in the first half
                  mile, is very modest and this is a
                  truly easy family ramble.
                  Coniston village is well provided
                  with shops and other facilities.
                  Attractions include Brantwood,
                  the former home of John
                  Ruskin, The National Trust
                  steam launch *Gondola*, the John
                  Ruskin Museum and a modest
                  memorial to the late Donald
                  Campbell (on the little green
                  close to the entrance to the
                  village car park) who died on
                  Coniston Water in 1956
                  attempting to break the world

The Tale of Two Bad Mice

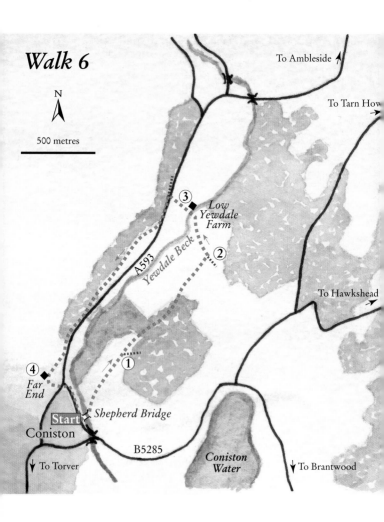

Walk 6

N

500 metres

To Ambleside

To Tarn How

Low
Yewdale
Farm

③

②

A593

Yewdale Beck

To Hawkshead

①

④
Far
End

Shepherd Bridge

Start
Coniston

B5285

↓ To Torver

Coniston
Water

↓ To Brantwood

water speed record. His boat, Bluebird, capsized at approximately 300 mph.

REFRESHMENTS   None *en route*, but Coniston village has inns, including the Black Bull, home of the locally brewed Bluebird bitter, and cafes. A short distance along the road to Ambleside is Yew Tree Farm, with walkers' tea room, originally encouraged by Beatrix Potter (WALK 5).

CAR PARKING   There are spaces on the road that bypasses the village centre and which connects the A593, Ambleside to Coniston road with the B5285, Coniston to Hawkshead road, close to Shepherd Bridge, grid reference 305978.

MAP   Ordnance Survey Explorer OL7, The English Lakes, south-eastern area, 1:25,000.

THE WALK

Start Leave the public road along a broad track; there is a 'public footpath' sign and a seat at the junction. Cross Yewdale Beck, a principal feeder of Coniston Water, immediately on an attractive old bridge. Turn left over a waymarked stile in a few metres, then through a kissing gate in a further 25m to follow a well-worn path across farming land, passing a group of mature oak trees.

① Go through a kissing gate beside an unusual building, a Gothic folly dated 1855. Inside the building are benches and information boards concerning the Marshall family and the Monk Coniston estate. The building was apparently purpose-built for foxhounds. The path rises steadily and there are soon views of Coniston Water, Coniston Old Man and the nearer Yewdale Fell. Go through a farm gate to continue, passing through a thicket of gorse. Go through a kissing gate to pass through coniferous woodland, part of Back Guards Plantation. Leave the woodland through another kissing gate and pass through another gate to continue over grass to a waymark on a post. Bear left here, under an oak tree, then through a waymarked gateway, descending to a waymarked gate/stile.

② Join a lane, at a 'Low Yewdale, Tarn Hows' signpost, turning left. Reach a

Cottages at Far End Farm

1. Beatrix Potter
purchased this farm as part
of the Monk Coniston
estate, in partnership with
the National Trust, in
1930. She retained
ownership of it when the
farms and land were
divided between herself
and the Trust.

'Tilberthwaite, High Yewdale,
Coniston' signpost, cross Yewdale Beck
again, and reach another signpost
'Coniston, Tilberthwaite' in 20m. The
attractive Low Yewdale farmstead is to
the right, with a bank barn beside the
track.[1] Walk along the farm access
drive to the A593 in less than 100m.
③ Go straight across the road to join
a 'permitted bridleway' through a gate.

Turn left. There is a signpost 'Coniston ¾ mile'. The gravelled path rises and falls very little as it heads back to Coniston along the bottom fringe of the wooded hillside. There are three bridges crossing little streams and a view of a former limekiln across a field to the left. The path forks in about three-quarters of a mile. Keep right, slightly uphill to a little gate. Continue along the bottom of the open fellside, soon passing above the backs of property at Far End. Look out for an unsignposted farm gate on the left; turn left here to descend to the Far End public road in about 40m. To the right are some of the outbuildings of the former Far End Farm.[2]

④ Join the road, turning right. The former farmhouse is well concealed to the right. Continue along the road, soon passing Holly How, a long-established youth hostel. At the crossroads go straight across to return to the parking area.

2. Again purchased by Beatrix as part of the Monk Coniston transaction and retained by her following the share-out with the National Trust. She was very annoyed when the Medical Officer of Health employed by the local council, Dr Patterson, visited the farm and commented adversely on the state of the shippon. Together with his colleague the Sanitary Inspector, he was trying to raise the generally low standards of the buildings in which many farm animals (and often their human keepers) were housed in the 1930s.

7.
HIGH ARNSIDE

DISTANCE
5½ km. (3½ miles). A visit to High Oxenfell Farm adds approximately 1 km (⅔ mile). The ascent of Black Crag adds approximately 1½ km (1 mile).

DESCRIPTION
A very pleasant circuit around some of the comparatively gentle countryside of south-eastern Lakeland, using minor roadways and excellent tracks, up and down but without serious ascent. Much of the route is through the Monk Coniston estate, purchased by Beatrix Potter in 1930, in partnership with the National Trust. Beatrix retained ownership of half of the estate and managed the remainder for several years as at that time the Trust did not have a local agent. The farms at High Arnside, High and Low Oxenfell were all part of the estate.

The Tale of Mr. Tod

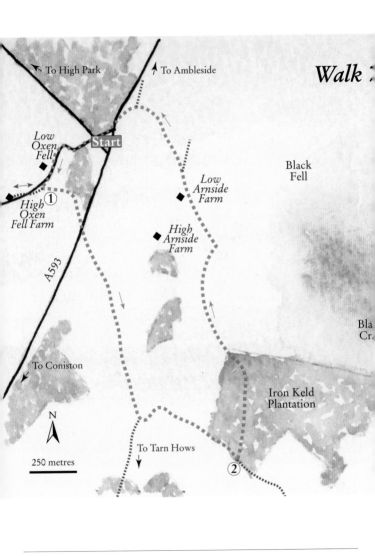

To High Park ←

↑ To Ambleside

Walk ?

Low Oxen Fell ◼

Start

Black Fell

Low Arnside Farm ◆

High Oxen Fell Farm ◼◼ ①

High Arnside Farm ◆

A593

Bla Cr.

To Coniston ↙

Iron Keld Plantation

N ↑

250 metres

To Tarn Hows ↓

②

THE WALK

1. This is listed as part of the Monk Coniston estate. It is now an old house rather than a farm, but the adjacent fields are pure Beatrix Potter farming country. Whether as owner or as agent for the National Trust, Beatrix had a strongly 'hands on' attitude to managing her properties. She concerned herself with every detail of walling, fencing, repairs to property and the well-being of the animals. She was strongly motivated by the need to preserve traditional landscapes, farming methods and the way of life. Without using the word herself, she was one of the earliest true conservationists.

Start Facing the National Trust notice, start along the left hand of the two surfaced roadways, soon descending to cross a stream, then rising through mixed woodland. There are splendid views, including Lingmoor and Wetherlam. Low Oxenfell is soon reached.[1]

(1) In a further 200m reach a junction, (to visit the pretty farm at High Oxenfell continue along the same roadway for about 300m then return to the junction). If not visiting High Oxenfell, turn sharp left along another surfaced roadway, rising initially. Continue as far as the main road. Go straight across to a surfaced road rising past a bungalow 'Mole End'. In 250m the road bends to the left to 'High Arnside Farm only'. Go straight ahead at this point, along a broad stony track 'public bridleway to Knipe Fold, footpath to Tarn Hows'. The excellent track, a little up and down, crosses a stream. To the left is light woodland, to the right are mountain views. Pass the start of a footpath leading to Tarn Hows.

When the Trust
eventually appointed
an agent to take over
management of its
property in the Lake
District, including its
share of the Monk
Coniston estate, it was
hardly surprising that
Beatrix considered
him to be quite
incapable of
maintaining the
standards which she
had set. A series of
letters from Beatrix
to the Trust's
headquarters in
London reveals
her increasing
exasperation with
his actions and
his personality.

Continue towards 'Iron Keld and
Hawkshead', rising. There is a
glimpse of Tarn Hows to the right.
② Turn left at a kissing gate,
signposted 'Black Crag, Arnside' and
rise through the National Trust Iron
Keld plantation, a little sparse after

High Oxen Fell Farm

recent felling. Go through a gate at the top of the plantation, soon enjoying fine views ahead, with the Langdale Pikes dominant. (Approximately half a kilometre – one third of a mile – to the right is the elusive summit of Black Crag,

a hill of 322m (1057ft) height and a good viewpoint. There are unofficial paths from our track to and from this summit). Continue along the well-defined track, through another gate, soon beginning a long descent. High Arnside Farm is away to the left, hidden from view. Pass close to Low Arnside Farm; High Arnside can now be seen on higher ground, above the rooftops of the lower farm. At a signposted fork keep left; at another fork in 40m keep left again, descending over grass to a gate. Approach another gate but do not go through. Bear left to pass through woodland and reach the main road. Cross over to return to the parking place.

High Arnside Landscape

8.

WRAY CASTLE

DISTANCE	5km (3 miles)
DESCRIPTION	Part out and back, part circuit, this is a very easy walk along a lovely section of the shore of England's largest lake. Since the imposition in 2005 of a speed limit on the lake, this is now an altogether more peaceful area. Underfoot there are no problems, most of the way being along a broad track.
	Wray Castle is an impressive sham, built in the 1840s by an eccentric Liverpool doctor. Owned by the National Trust, it was used for many years as a training centre for marine communications.
REFRESHMENTS	Take a picnic

The Tale of the Flopsy Bunnies

Walk 8

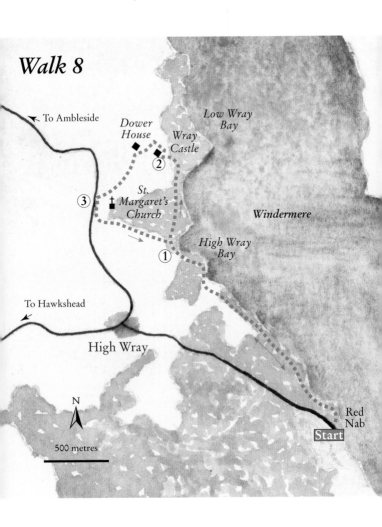

To Ambleside

Dower House

Wray Castle

Low Wray Bay

②

St. Margaret's Church

③

Windermere

High Wray Bay

①

To Hawkshead

High Wray

N

500 metres

Red Nab

Start

CAR PARKING	Red Nab car park, accessed from the Ambleside to Hawkshead road, via High Wray, grid reference 385995.
MAP	Ordnance Survey Explorer OL7, The English Lakes, south-eastern area, 1:25,000.
THE WALK	**Start** Leave the car park along the broad lakeside track to the north, passing a vehicular barrier and entering woodland which is part of the Claiffe Estate, owned by the National Trust. The views across the lake include much of the celebrated 'Fairfield Horseshoe' of mountains. Also in view are historic Calgarth Park, White Cross Bay, home of a factory manufacturing Sunderland flying boats in World War II, the National Park Visitor Centre at Brockhole, the Langdale Chase Hotel and the Low Wood Hotel, Wansfell Pike, above Ambleside, is prominent.[1]

1. The Low Wood Hotel was recorded by Beatrix as 'clean and dull' when she visited in 1886.

PREVIOUS PAGE
High Wray Church

LEFT
Wray Castle

Pass a boathouse and cross a stream on a plank bridge before reaching High Wray Bay, with another boathouse. Leave the Claiffe Estate through a gate, signposted 'public bridleway, Wray Church'. Go through another gate, the track now rising gently.

① In a further 40m turn right, through a gate signposted 'permitted footpath Wray Castle, National Trust Wray Castle Estate'. Continue over grass, a fine area for lakeside picnics, soon passing a third boathouse before reaching the wooded knoll on which Wray Castle stands. Bear left to ascend a steep little slope between the trees. At the top of the slope bear right to head for a gate/stile. A few metres before the gate/stile, turn left, uphill, towards the castle. Go through a gate to join the castle roadway. Pass a vehicular 'way out' sign to reach the castle terrace, a fine viewpoint.[2]

2. Wray Castle was the Potter family's first Lake District holiday home, in 1882, when their favourite house at Dalguise in Perthshire was not available. Beatrix, who was sixteen years old, much enjoyed rambling in the surrounding countryside. In her Journal she recorded visits to Hawkshead and the remains of Hawkshead Hall, One visit to Hawkshead was an adventure – she was continually lost, asked the way three times, got stuck in stiles, was chased by cows and alarmed by collies at every farm. Other excursions included Patterdale, Stock Ghyll Force at Ambleside and the local Harvest Festival. She was fond of nearby Blelham Tarn, which she records as having been a source of fish for the monks at Furness Abbey. (Hawkshead Hall was an outlying 'grange' of that great abbey). Of immense importance to Beatrix's later life as a farmer and conservationist was her meeting with Hardwicke (later Canon) Rawnsley

who was at that time vicar of St Margaret's, the parish church of High Wray, adjacent to the castle. Rawnsley soon became a friend of the family, impressing them with his powerful advocacy on the vital need to conserve the fragile Lakeland landscape. One of the three founder members of the National Trust in 1895, he was also heavily involved in the formation of the Lake District Defence League, forerunner of the present day Friends of the Lake District. The teenage Beatrix could hardly fail to be impressed by Rawnsley. The friendship continued after he moved to Crosthwaite Church, Keswick, when the Potter family had several holidays at Fawe Park and Lingholm, both close to Derwentwater. Her father, Rupert Potter, became one of the first life members of the National Trust.

② Continue along the castle access road, passing the Dower House before reaching the public road by the gatehouse.
③ Turn left at the road and then left again along a signposted bridleway in a few metres. St Margaret's Church is on the left. A good track descends, with a stream on the right, to rejoin the outward route by the gate at point 1. Bear right to return along the lakeside track to the car park.

9.
COCKSHOTT POINT, BOWNESS

DISTANCE	2km (1¼ miles).
DESCRIPTION	An entirely easy little walk, strolling along the Glebe, Bowness's lakeside promenade, followed by a track to National Trust-owned Cockshott Point, with the return across fields, passing the former rectory, the pitch and putt course and the cemetery. The whole route is close to the many shops and visitor attractions of Bowness. Firm surfaces underfoot throughout.
REFRESHMENTS	Boatman's Café, inns, ice cream and other refreshments along the Glebe, Bowness.
CAR PARKING	Small parking area on the cul-de-sac approach road to the Boatman's Café and the coach park, grid reference 401967, or find a roadside space along the Glebe. Ordnance

The Tale of Peter Rabbit

Walk 9

Windermere

Steamboat
Museum

To
Winderm

A5074

St.
Martin's
Church

Bowness
Bay

World of
Beatrix
Potter

Belle
Isle

House

Start

Pitch
and
Putt

①

Cockshott
Point

Cemetery

Rectory

②

A592

A5074

N

500 metres

Ferry

To
Newby
Bridge

Lindeth
Howe

MAP

Survey Explorer OL7, The English Lakes, south-eastern area, 1:25,000.

THE WALK

Start From the car park walk to the Glebe and turn left to continue by the side of the lake (Windermere), passing several boating and other commercial premises. The views up the lake to the mountains of the Fairfield Horseshoe are superb.

① As the road bends to the left, go straight ahead, through a gate, along a track among the trees 'leading to Cockshott Point'. The track is broad and easy. As the lake shore is reached there are fine picnic sites and views across to the well-wooded Claiffe Heights and to Belle Isle with its historic circular house.[1] Continue along the path, towards the public slipway and the ferry terminal, passing many moored boats.[2]

1. In 1927 there was a possibility of the Cockshott Point area of land being sold for development. Beatrix Potter was prominent in helping to raise funds for purchase of the land by the National Trust so that it could be retained for public access in perpetuity. Although by this time her eyesight was not good she produced fifty drawings based on illustrations from *The Tale of Peter Rabbit* for use as greetings cards. These were sold at a guinea each to her friends in the United States of America, the proceeds going to the appeal, which was successful.

② Go through a kissing gate to join another track. Turn left and go through another kissing gate; the house on the left is the former rectory, with several traditional 'Lake District' chimney stacks. After the track narrows, go through another kissing gate to joint the public road. Go almost straight across to continue along Rectory Road, between the cemetery and the pitch and putt course, leading directly to the car parking area.[3]

2. Beatrix was a frequent user of the ferry, particularly after her father died, when her mother moved from London to a house on Longtail Hill at the Storrs end of Bowness, now the Lindeth Howe Hotel. In 1912, the use of the lake by noisy seaplanes caused local concern, exacerbated by a proposal to build a factory for the manufacture of the planes by the side of the lake.

Bowness

Beatrix organised a petition against this proposal, pointing out the danger of the noise frightening the horses being conveyed by the ferry boat. The seaplanes went elsewhere.

3. The World of Beatrix Potter is approximately a quarter of a mile distant on Crag Brow, Bowness. This visitor attraction comprises a comprehensive exhibition of the Beatrix Potter characters in tableau scenes, with video display, shop and café, superb for children and with plenty of interest for adults. In 2006, a bronze sculpture by Anthony Bennet was unveiled on the terrace at the lower end of the premises. The statue depicts three children, a host of Beatrix Potter characters, a farm and some words in code from her Journal.

Sculpture outside World of Beatrix Potter

10.
TROUTBECK PARK FARM

DISTANCE   9km (5½ miles)

DESCRIPTION   A basically level circular walk
                    entirely within the spacious
                    Troutbeck Valley, visiting the
                    important Beatrix Potter farm at
                    Troutbeck Park. Troutbeck
                    village is a linear stringing
                    together of five hamlets along
                    the lower slopes of Wansfell Pike,
                    at the level where water emerges
                    from the hillside, as evidenced by
                    the named 'wells' along the
                    village road. There is a great
                    array of traditional farm
                    buildings, largely dating from the
                    late 17th and early 18th
                    centuries, when the profitability
                    of wool provided a good deal of
                    local wealth. The National Trust
                    property at Townend is the
                    typical home of a yeoman
                    farmer ('statesman') of the time.
                    Troutbeck Church has an

The Tale of Pigling Bland

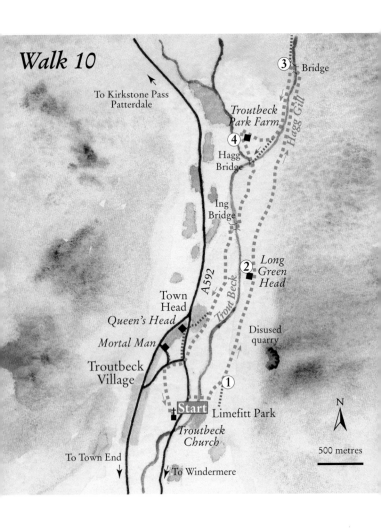

Walk 10

To Kirkstone Pass
Patterdale

③ Bridge

*Troutbeck
Park Farm*

Hagg Gill

④

Hagg
Bridge

Ing
Bridge

*Long
Green
Head*

②

A592

Trout Beck

Town
Head

Queen's Head

Mortal Man

Disused
quarry

Troutbeck
Village

①

Start

Limefitt Park

*Troutbeck
Church*

N

To Town End

To Windermere

500 metres

unusually large and very fine east window, the work of the pre-Raphaelite artists Burne-Jones, Madox-Brown and Morris.

REFRESHMENTS   The Queen's Head Inn and the Mortal Man Inn, with its famous sign, are both short diversions from the line of the walk.

CAR PARKING   Roadside layby for three cars on the A592, about 100m north of Troutbeck Church, grid reference 414029. Alternatively there is a small parking area at the foot of the little road which leads from Church Bridge on the A592 up to the main part of the village, a short distance to the south of the church.

MAP   Ordnance Survey Explorer OL7, The English Lakes, south-eastern area, 1:25,000.

THE WALK   Start Start along the roadside, turning right into the entrance to the Limefitt Park camping and

caravan site in 100m. There is a public right of way through this property. Walk down the access roadway and cross the bridge over Trout Beck. There is a blue arrow bridleway waymark on a post. Pass a junction, going straight ahead, with the camping field on the left, to head for the Haybarn Inn, passing another waymark. Go up a few steps to a signpost, indicating a left turn, above the Inn. Rise gently to a waymarked gate and follow a track which joins a more major track in about 100m.

① Fork left to continue along the valley side, passing above a plantation. In a further 50m the remains of a long defunct ski lift can be seen on the left. Across the valley is Wansfell Pike.[1] Go through a farm gate and continue up the valley. For much of the way, this track follows the division between the comparatively scarce and valuable valley bottom land to the left and the rough bracken-covered hillside to the right. Ahead is The Tongue, the steep end of a ridge which divides the upper part of the valley. Behind The Tongue, Stony Cove Pike and High Street are the higher mountains.[2]

1. The broad track known as Nanny Lane rises above Troutbeck village, across the flank of the mountain. In August and September, 1895, whilst on a family holiday at Holehird, Beatrix spent time rambling along this lane, looking for fossils. On the same holiday she also fossil-hunted at Sour Howes Quarry, up the hillside to the right of our track.

2. In one of her letters Beatrix tells the story of losing one of her farm dogs somewhere on The Tongue. She spent many hours clambering over the rough steep ground in a fruitless attempt to find the lost animal.

②   Pass through Long Green Head Farm to continue along the farm access roadway. The high ridge to the right has, in succession, the peaks of Yoke, Ill Bell and Froswick. Cross a bridge over a small stream then, as the farm roadway bends to the left, go straight ahead. Go through a gate, pass an isolated farm building and cross a tumbling stream. The wall on the left is now very much the intake wall, marking the highest limit to which generations of farmers have been able to improve and use land. A few foxgloves brighten the generally sparse vegetation. Continue through a waymarked gate, up the branch of the valley drained by Hagg Gill. Pass below the spoil heaps of a long disused quarry, then an isolated building, before crossing the gill on a bridge and rising to a gate and a junction with another track, the lower part of the Roman route to High Street.

③   Turn sharp left, going through a waymarked gate to follow the delightful broad track towards Troutbeck Park Farm. There are more gates and a short cut footpath with a kissing gate on the left before the farm is reached. At the farm go left between the buildings and then left again in front of the house before turning right to continue along the farm access road. The farm dogs are likely to make a great deal of noise.[3]

④ Continue along the farm access roadway, flanked by descendants of Beatrix's Herdwick sheep in the adjacent fields. Cross Hagg Bridge and then Ing Bridge. At a signposted junction turn left along a bridleway, a good track largely between stone walls, with foxgloves, campion and ransomes. (From this junction the Queen's Head Inn may be reached by continuing along the roadway). Go straight across the main road and follow a minor road for about 200m to another signposted junction. (To visit the Mortal Man Inn make a short diversion to the right. To go to the main part of the village go straight ahead). To continue the circuit turn left, soon reaching a kissing gate. A narrow, grassy path heads towards the church, largely between fences. Reach a little lane close to the church, turning left to the main road, then left again to the parking layby.

3. The purchase of this farm in 1924 was of great significance to Beatrix. Having farmed on a relatively small scale in and around Near Sawrey since 1905, she now had the desire, the financial resources and the experience to take on a much larger farm (about 2000 acres) such as Troutbeck Park. The farm was in a poor, rundown condition with liver fluke rife among the stock of sheep. Beatrix was typically resolute in meeting the challenge, taking the opportunity to develop her interest in pure-bred Herdwick sheep. She was specific in her requirements – the landlord's stock to comprise 700 ewes, 180 'twinters' (two winters – two years old) and 220 hoggs (male or female lambs before first

Queens Head Inn

shearing). She lured a very able farmer, Tom Storey, from his nearby employment by an offer of double wages to manage the farm. Between them they used a new pharmaceutical product to cure the fluke, building up a flock of Herdwicks which could compete successfully at local shows throughout the district. Beatrix built a new shepherd's house – to the right of the original farmhouse – and used a room in the farmhouse (to the left of the front door) as her local office. She came over from Near Sawrey several times each week. Having acquired a motor car, she was driven by her driver/handyman. From the outset she intended to leave the farm to the National Trust as a permanent safeguard against the developers who had been showing interest in building on the more accessible parts of the land.

11.

THE AMATEUR LAND AGENT

DISTANCE   5½ km (3½ miles)

DESCRIPTION   A circuit mainly in the
Tilberthwaite valley, with its
history of extensive quarrying.
Present-day activity is greatly
reduced and nature has concealed
much of the evidence. The great
excavation near to Hodge Close
remains as an awesome reminder
of the extent of this industry over
a period of two hundred years.
Coupled with Beatrix Potter
farming land (four farms) at both
ends of the route, this area is now
attractive to walk. The route is
almost entirely over good,
easy tracks.

REFRESHMENTS   None en route, but a diversion to
visit the Three Shires Inn in
Little Langdale adds a little more
than one kilometre to the circuit.

The Tale of Benjamin Bunny

To Three
Shires Inn

*Little Langdale
Tarn*

Little Langdale Beck

Slater
Bridge

Bridge
and ford

② ③

*Stang End
Farm*

*Moss Rigg
Wood*

Walk 11

*Hodge
Close*

Old quarry

*High
Tilberthwaite
Farm*

①

*Low
Tilberthwaite
Farm*

④

Cottages

*Holme
Ground
Farm*

Holme Fell

Start

N

500 metres

To Coniston

CAR PARKING	Car park close to Yewdale Beck, reached by the little Tilberthwaite road which leaves the Ambleside to Coniston road (A593) less than two miles north of Coniston village, grid reference 305011.
MAP	Ordnance Survey Explorer OL7, The English Lakes, south-eastern area, 1:25,000.
THE WALK	**Start** Turn left from the car park, cross Yewdale Beck, and head for Low Tilberthwaite Farm and cottages. The farm has a good example of the Lakeland 'spinning gallery'.[1] Continue along the access roadway to High Tilberthwaite Farm, entered through a gate with a 'public bridleway' sign. This farm was likewise part of the Monk Coniston estate, passing to the National Trust in the same way as its neighbour.

1. Beatrix Potter bought Low Tilberthwaite in 1930 in partnership with the National Trust, as part of the Monk Coniston estate. Ownership passed to the Trust, but Beatrix managed the farm and several others on their behalf for several years. She regarded herself as an 'amateur land agent' but nothing was left to chance in her thorough and detailed management of a large number of properties. However, when the local Council

① After the farm, the roadway loses its tarmac surface, rising

Medical Officer of Health and the Sanitary Inspector were later inspecting rural properties, she remarked that the sanitation at this farm and cottages was 'not nice'.

gently, soon passing the first quarry spoil heaps, which are below to the right. Go through a kissing gate, then a farm gate, passing close to long-abandoned quarries. At a fork, bear right, downhill, to pass below Moss Rigg wood. A track joins from the right; bear left to continue, soon passing Brooklands bungalow.

② At a signposted junction the route turns sharp right to follow 'Colwith and Skelwith'. However, a few metres further is Little Langdale Beck, with a ford and footbridge, an attractive place for a picnic and the start of the possible extension of the walk to visit the Three Shires Inn, a straightforward route along the lane

Low Tilberthwaite Farm

2. Stang End Farm was
another part of the Monk
Coniston purchase, with
close-grouped buildings
and a 'spinning gallery'.
Beatrix retained
ownership in this case,
the farm passing to the
National Trust after her
death. When the
sanitation was under
consideration, she
remarked that fifteen
people were using one
earth closet!

on the far side of the bridge. With or without diversions, continue by heading for Colwith and Skelwith at the fork, crossing Pierce How Beck before rising steeply along a surfaced roadway to Stang End Farm. The views over Little Langdale from the higher ground are splendid, including Lingmoor and mighty Bowfell, with Wetherlam well to the left.[2]

③ Turn right at the farm at a junction signposted to 'Hodge Close', rising along a tarmac road. The road soon loses its surface. Go through a farm gate and continue to another gate as the track bears to the right to enter woodland. Cross a little stream and rise past a wooden building to reach Wyke House. Go through a gate to enter Hodge Close hamlet, with abundant evidence of the former industry. Continue along the tarmac Hodge Close access road, rising to pass close to the tremendous excavation, with its

Old quarry near Hodge Close

3. Like the two Tilberthwaite farms, after the joint Monk Coniston purchase, Holme Ground passed at once to the National Trust, Beatrix continuing as manager. There is a typical Lakeland bank barn.

deep pool. Danger notices are displayed! The Langdale Pikes are in view. Pass a row of cottages, probably built for the quarrymen but now more likely to be holiday homes, before reaching Holme Ground Farm.[3]

④ Immediately after passing the farm, turn right. There is a 'public footpath to

Holme Ground Farm

High Tilberthwaite' sign. Go through a
farm gate and continue over grass, with
High Tilberthwaite farm in view ahead.
Bear right, downhill, to head for a gate
beside a wall. Go through and enter the
farmyard through another gate. Turn left
to return along the outward route to
the car park.

12.
LITTLE LANGDALE

DISTANCE

6½ km (4 miles).

DESCRIPTION

This circuit of Little Langdale starts and finishes in Great Langdale. Whilst classified as an easy walk, with no hills or mountains to climb, it does have more rise and fall than most walks in the book and some lengths of footpath are quite minor, with rough ground underfoot. There are several stiles and Little Langdale Beck is crossed on (easy) stepping stones. Little Langdale is much the quieter, less frequented, of the two Langdale valleys. Beatrix Potter had a considerable presence here, three of her farms being included in the route of the walk, with three others in view.

REFRESHMENTS

The celebrated Brittania Inn at Elterwater is a few metres from the start/finish of the walk. The

The Tale of Timmy Tiptoes

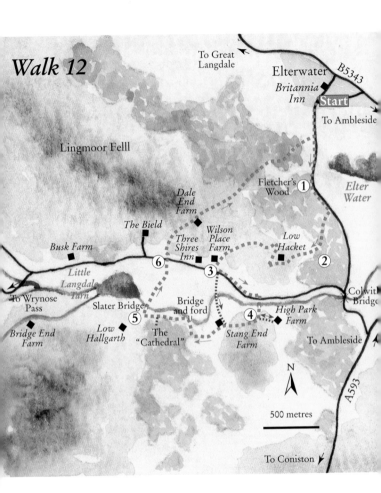

Walk 12

To Great
Langdale

B5343

Elterwater

*Britannia
Inn*

Start

To Ambleside

Lingmoor Felll

Fletcher's
Wood ①

*Elter
Water*

*Dale
End
Farm*

The Bield

Busk Farm

*Three
Shires
Inn*

*Wilson
Place
Farm*

*Low
Hacket*

②

⑥

③

Colwit
Bridge

*Little
Langdale
Tarn*

To Wrynose
Pass

Slater Bridge

*Bridge
and ford*

④

*High Park
Farm*

To Ambleside

*Bridge End
Farm*

*Low
Hallgarth*

⑤

The
"Cathedral"

*Stang End
Farm*

To Coniston →

A593

N

500 metres

Three Shires Inn at Little Langdale hamlet is about 400m diversion from the line of the walk. The Eltermere Country House Hotel at Elterwater offers a bar, afternoon teas and other refreshments.

CAR PARKING

National Trust car park at Elterwater village, grid reference 328048.

MAP

Ordnance Survey Explorer OL7, The English Lakes, south-eastern area, 1:25,000.

THE WALK

Start Turn left out of the car park, cross Great Langdale Beck, and continue along the minor road. Pass the youth hostel and then Eltermere Country House Hotel. Go straight ahead at a junction, heading for 'Colwith and Little Langdale'. There is a glimpse of Elterwater to the left. Reach woodland, the National Trust-owned Fletcher's Wood.

① At a junction with a drive on the right, and a stile beside, turn right, then left immediately to follow a good track which stays parallel with

1. Beatrix Potter's farms at
High Park and Stang End
can be seen across the valley.

the road for approximately 400m.
On reaching another track, with a
gate and signposts immediately to the
left, turn right to rise along a broad
path through the woodland, with
beech predominant. The path
narrows, but is always clear on the
ground. Go over a stile at the top, to
leave the wood and continue over
grass, still rising. Go under a large oak,
with a wall on the right. Cross the
occasional little stream before
reaching the access drive to Low
Hackett Farm (waymark on post).
② Turn right to walk along the
drive, rising past a farm outbuilding
to reach a gate. Go through. Before
reaching the farm buildings turn left
(waymark on post). Go over a stile
and follow the waymarks to the right
to by-pass the farm. The fine views
include much of the Little Langdale
valley, with the great bulk of
Wetherlam dominant.[1] Continue
over a stile beside the right-hand of
two gates (waymark behind stile). The
route is now left across a meadow, not
very evident on the ground, heading

for a gap in a wall. Cross another large, sloping meadow, keeping a little to the left of a tree plantation. The Wrynose Pass is prominent ahead. Go between rushes to a small gate, with a little signpost, a few steps down and a ditch. Go left, then over a stile in 40m to continue the descent. A broad grass track winds its way down to Wilson Place Farm. Go through a farm gate to reach tarmac. Turn left to walk to the public road in 40m.

③ Turn left to follow the road for about 500m, passing the start of the short-cut footpath to Stang End Farm and then a terrace of cottages. The road goes downhill; at the bottom turn right through a little gate with a 'public footpath' sign. Descend the bank of Little Langdale Beck, into woodland. Cross the beck on generous stepping stones and bear left up the steep opposite bank, where there may be slippery mud. Go over a stile at the top of the bank and rise steeply up a meadow, initially through rushes. Head for a farm gate/stile at the top.

④ Join a farm access road, turning left for about 100m to go to High Park Farm.[2] Return to point 4 and continue along the farm road, with views across large swathes of Beatrix Potter farming country, little changed since 1930. Across the valley, Lingmoor is the long ridge, with the knobble of Side Pike at its western end. Walk down to Stang End Farm, also

2. It is part of the Monk Coniston estate purchased by Beatrix in partnership with the National Trust in 1930. The farm is beautifully situated, with fine views across the valley.

Slater Bridge

visited on WALK 11. The bank barn, with spinning gallery, is unusual in having entrances to both levels on one side. The short cut footpath terminates at Stang End. Continue downhill, passing a gate/cattle grid before crossing Pierce How Beck. Turn right immediately, along a path through the woodland, bearing left to walk close to Little Langdale Beck for a short distance. Reach a broad track, turning right to the ford/footbridge which crosses the beck. Do not cross; go straight ahead along another broad, gravel track, soon with quarry spoil heaps adjacent. Go through a farm gate. Slater Bridge is now visible to the right. In 60m a path climbing as a diversion to the left leads to a great quarry feature – the 'Cathedral'– in a few metres.

⑤ In a further 50m turn right through a kissing gate and go over a stile to reach the delightful bridge. Cross over and follow a rising path,

Busk House Farm,
Little Langdale

The Bield,
Little Langdale

3. For many years this
was the home of
celebrated sculptress
Josefina de Vasconcellos
and her husband,
painter Delmar Banner,
good friends of Beatrix.

keeping to the left of the wall at two
junctions (follow an 'Elterwater' sign
at the second). From the top of this
path there are views of Little
Langdale Tarn and Beatrix Potter's
farms at, from the left, Low Hallgarth,
Bridge End (hard to spot among trees)
and Busk. Fell Foot Farm, which was
not purchased by Beatrix, is also in
view. This farm has a platform,
believed to be a Norse 'Ting
Mound' meeting place at the rear.
Almost ahead the pink-washed
form of 'The Beild' stands out.[3]

Dale End Farm

Go through a kissing gate, then a farm gate, to pass High Birk Howe Farm, soon reaching the public road. The Three Shires Inn is a 400m diversion to the right.

⑥ Turn left, then right in 10m along a tarmac farm road 'Unsuitable for Motor Vehicles' to rise steadily to Dale End Farm.[4] The road loses its surface but continues to rise. Go through a

4. Another farm purchased in 1930 by Beatrix.

farm gate and along a level section before commencing the long descent towards Elterwater. There is a rough, stony section of the broad track. At a fork immediately after a farm gate go straight ahead to continue the descent. Elterwater comes into view. Pass Elterwater Hall and join the public road. Turn left to return to the car park along the outward route.

13.
DERWENTWATER WEST SHORE

DISTANCE   4 km (2½ miles).

DESCRIPTION   A delightful walk, largely along
                        the shore of what is arguably
                        the most attractive of all the
                        lakes, generally level, along
                        broad easy tracks without stiles
                        and with spectacular mountain
                        and lake views. Using the
                        Keswick Launch to reach the
                        start and finish points adds to
                        the overall excursion. The route
                        of the walk passes by two of the
                        Potter family holiday homes,
                        Lingholm (nine visits between
                        1885 and 1907) and Fawe Park
                        (1903). Beatrix sketched and
                        painted a great deal during
                        these holidays, as evidenced by
                        her Derwentwater sketchbook.
                            For many years the Keswick
                        Launch Company has used
                        traditional wooden boats to
                        provide a service round the

The Tale of Squirrel Nutkin

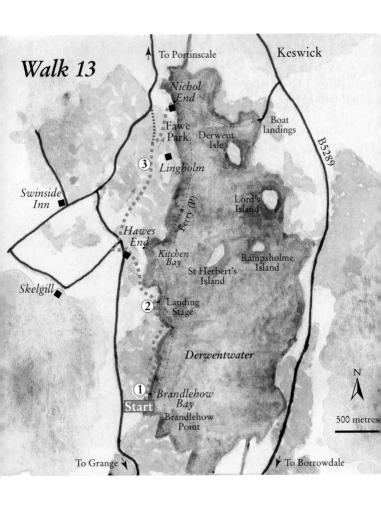

Walk 13

Keswick

To Portinscale

Nichol End

Boat landings

Fawe Park

Derwent Isle

③

Lingholm

B5289

Swinside Inn

Lord's Island

Ferry (P)

Hawes End

Kitchen Bay

Rampsholme Island

St Herbert's Island

Skelgill

②

Landing Stage

Derwentwater

N

① **Start**   *Brandlehow Bay*

Brandlehow Point

500 metres

To Grange ↙   ↘ To Borrowdale

lake, alternating clockwise and anti-clockwise journeys. There are seven landing jetties in addition to the base at Keswick. The summer (Good Friday to the end of September) timetable provides a half-hourly service, with extra sailings during the peak holiday period. In winter the service is more restricted.

REFRESHMENTS
Café at Nichol End. The Swinside Inn is approximately one kilometre from the end of the walk. Café and inns at Portinscale.

CAR PARKING
Large pay and display public car park beside the Theatre by the Lake, accessed from the Keswick to Borrowdale road, B5289, grid reference 265229.

MAP
Ordnance Survey Explorer OL4, The English Lakes, north-western area, 1:25,000.

THE WALK

Start Leave the boat at High Brandlehow jetty. There is a National Trust sign and a few picnic tables.

① Turn right to follow a well-used track through the woodland by the edge of the lake, soothed by the gentle lapping of the water on the

'Owl Island'

1. St Herbert's Island became 'Owl Island' in Beatrix Potter's *The Tale of Squirrel Nutkin*. It was the residence of old Mr Brown who gave permission for the squirrels to collect nuts on his island and who punished Nutkin for his persistent insolence. Her Derwentwater sketchbook has several portrayals of the island, which has changed little over the ensuing years.

shore. Across the lake Walla Crag is in view. Pass the tiny Withensike Bay. The views along the lake include St Herbert's Island, with little Latrigg, behind Keswick, and mighty Blencathra, to the right, providing a backdrop.

St Herbert was a 7th century hermit, resident on the island for many years, a friend of the legendary St Cuthbert. It is claimed that he expressed a wish to die at the same time as his friend. The wish was apparently granted on 20th March 687.[1] The track continues over three little bridges, crossing streams, before reaching Victoria Bay, then the jetty at Low Brandlehow.

② Go through the gate behind the jetty, then immediately fork left, passing through more open country to another gate, with Skiddaw coming more fully into view. Pass a 'public footpath

Lingholm Keswick' sign then a huge dated log carved into seats. At another gate join a tarmac roadway, turning right to walk to Hawes End Centre, a large property with car park. Ignore the path to Hawes End jetty and a private road, instead turn right at a little gate to follow a broad path into woodland. After crossing a stream on a footbridge, cross an open meadow. Behind is probably the finest view of Catbells. Go through a gate to re-enter woodland, part of the extensive grounds of Lingholm. In a short distance there is open ground to the right with the house beyond. Unfortunately, only the chimneys and part of the roof are visible and there is no public access.[2]

(3) Go through a gate to reach the Lingholm access drive. Go straight across, passing a 'footpath Keswick Portinscale' sign. Keep right, downhill, at a

2. Lingholm was a favourite holiday home for the Potter family, who visited it nine times. During these periods of residence Beatrix drew and painted extensively.

She also saw many red squirrels
in the surrounding woodland.
A letter which she wrote to
Norah Moore, daughter of her
former governess, in September
1901 set out what became *The
Tale of Squirrel Nutkin*, published
in 1903.

Keswick Boat Landings

fork, soon passing behind Fawe Park.[3] Continue to the marina and the launch jetty at Nichol End, to return across the lake to Keswick. (It is possible to return to Keswick on foot, if preferred. From Nichol End, walk up to the public road, turning right to reach Portinscale. In the village turn right, passing a hotel, to head for an elegant bridge over the river; cross the bridge then, at a junction of paths, turn right to head for the centre of Keswick. Keep right, through the town, to head back to the car park).

3. This substantial house was the Potter family holiday home in 1903. Of particular significance is the kitchen garden, painted several times by Beatrix. She used it as the setting for Mr McGregor's garden in *The Tale of Benjamin Bunny*, published in 1904. This tale also includes her best-known character, Peter Rabbit, Benjamin's cousin. The two rabbits climb on to the top of a high brick wall before descending a pear tree to enter the garden in an attempt to recover Peter's clothes, put on to a scarecrow by Mr McGregor after Peter's adventures in the earlier *Tale of Peter Rabbit*. Fawe Park and its gardens are privately owned and only the upper part of the house is visible. However, it is possible to peep over/through the fence and much of what Beatrix painted as Mr McGregor's garden is still recognisable, particularly the high buttressed wall. The following year, when on holiday at nearby Lingholm, Beatrix herself remarked on the difficulty of viewing the Fawe Park gardens, presumably from the same track.

Hill Top in the style of Mr. McGregor's garden

Derwentwater scenes

Derwentwater

'Owl Island'

FOLLOWING PAGE
Derwentwater

14.
ON THE TRAIL OF
MRS. TIGGY-WINKLE

DISTANCE

9¾ km (6 miles). Shorter version
5¼ km (3¼ miles).

DESCRIPTION

A mainly level circuit exploring
the lovely Newlands Valley, using
good tracks. The mountain
views are superb. Beatrix Potter
sketched and painted in the
valley during the Potter family
holidays at nearby Fawe Park
(1903) and Lingholm (1904). The
Derwentwater Sketchbook of
1903, now at the Beatrix Potter
Gallery in Hawkshead, contains
many of her Newlands pictures.
The Tale of Mrs Tiggy-Winkle,
published in 1905, is set wholly
in the valley, using local scenes
as backgrounds in the
illustrations, with the use of
some artistic licence. This walk
visits those sites.

The Tale of Mrs. Tiggy-Winkle

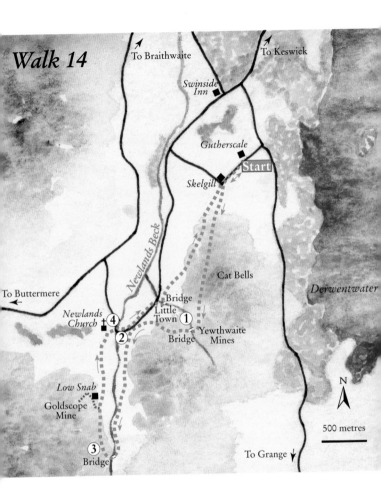

Walk 14

To Braithwaite

To Keswick

Swinside Inn

Gutherscale

Start

Skelgill

Newlands Beck

To Buttermere

Cat Bells

Derwentwater

Bridge

Newlands Church (4)

Little Town (1)

(2)

Bridge

Yewthwaite Mines

Low Snab

Goldscope Mine

(3)

Bridge

N

500 metres

To Grange

REFRESHMENTS	Pots of tea at Low Snab Farm. The Swinside Inn is reasonably close to the starting point of the walk.
CAR PARKING	Small car park along the minor road which leaves the Portinscale to Grange road, leading to Gutherscale and to Skelgill Farm, grid reference 247212. If full, there are roadside spaces by the Portinscale to Grange road.
MAP	Ordnance Survey Explorer OL4, The English Lakes, north-western area, 1:25,000.
THE WALK	**Start** Start along the little road mentioned above. Immediately before the gate which gives access to Skelgill Farm, fork left along a path rising above the farmstead. In previous centuries no less than three farms shared the meagre amount of usable land in this part of the valley. The fine track contours across the lower part of the Catbells

Skelgill Farm

hillside, with lovely views to Dale Head, Hindscarth and Robinson at the head of the valley and across to Causey Pike. The hamlet of Little Town comes into view before the former mining area around Yewthwaite Gill is reached.[1]

① The Gill is crossed on a footbridge. To reach the bridge there are alternative paths; the shorter keeps to the right of the main spoil heaps; the other, only a few metres longer, keeps to the left of the heaps before bearing right to the bridge, passing a

1. In *The Tale of Mrs Tiggy-Winkle* Beatrix has an illustration of Lucie running along this path, using artistic licence to include the buildings of Little Town, Church Bridge, Newlands Church and the rocky ridge descending steeply from Maiden Moor in her painting. The Derwentwater Sketchbook has a similar view up the valley, but without Lucie or the buildings.

Newlands Church

well-sealed mine entrance on the way. Continue along the track towards Little Town, soon passing above the hamlet.

② A right turn just after passing above the buildings provides the shorter version of the route, connecting with the return track in a few metres. For the full circuit continue along a narrow track through the bracken, soon joining the broad track which served the former Goldscope mine. As the spoil heaps of the former mine are approached, turn right by

Vale of Newlands,
Lucie's Path

2. Above the heaps a
mine entrance is
evident. This entrance
may well be Beatrix's
inspiration for the hole
in the hillside which
she illustrated as Mrs.
Tiggy-Winkles's home
and workplace in the
'Tale' of the same
name. It takes just a

the angle of a wall and cross an area of
rough ground on a rudimentary path
to reach a footbridge over the
Newlands Beck. Cross over, go through
a gate and rise to join a broad track.
③ Turn right to head for Low Snab
Farm. Above to the left are the great
spoil heaps.[2] Return to the circuit,
close to the gate giving access to Low
Snab Farm. As the notice states, this is
a permissive path, not a right of way.
Pass through the farm, exit by another
gate and continue along the farm
roadway to Newlands Church, prettily

little imagination to envisage a wooden door across the opening, as in the book. To reach the mine entrance, pass the foot of the spoil heaps and look for a little-used path which climbs through the bracken to join a better path; a left turn then leads to the mine. It is possible to walk for some distance inside the mine level but as in all mines great care should be taken.

set among trees. The former schoolroom which served the valley for ninety years, before finally closing in 1967, is attached to the church. The simple, well-proportioned little church is usually open for visitors.[3] Walk along the little road from the church, reaching a junction in 150m. ④ Turn right, cross Church Bridge, pass a car parking area and rise steadily along the road to Little Town.[4] At the far end of the hamlet turn right, along a broad track with a 'Skelgill 1 mile' sign. In 40m turn left through a farm gate, cross Yewthwaite Gill on a

3. The real 'Lucie', model for the child in *The Tale of Mrs Tiggy-Winkle*, was the daughter of the Newlands vicar in the early 20th century.

4. This is named by Beatrix as Lucie's home. However, the relevant illustration is a picture of Skelgill Farm.

Disused mine, home and workplace of Mrs. Tiggy-Winkle?

footbridge and follow a little lane. The great bulk of Skiddaw dominates the views ahead, with the little wooded hill of Swinside also prominent. Pass two more gates/stiles and a remotely sited house. Go through a kissing gate, the track now over grass. Reach a gate/ladder stile and pass through yet another gate before

5. Immediately to the left is the viewpoint which Beatrix used for the illustration in *The Tale of Mrs Tiggy-Winkle*, calling it 'Little-town'.

arriving at a gate/stile with a 'Skelgill Farm' sign. There is one more gate/stile before the farm buildings are reached. Join the tiny public road.[5] The route continues to the right, uphill, to a gate through which the outward route is rejoined. Turn left to return to the parking area.

15.
ESKDALE

DISTANCE	6½ km (4 miles).
DESCRIPTION	An attractive circular walk in the middle part of Eskdale, linking the foot of the well-known Hardknott Pass with the ancient farmstead of Brotherikeld, the Woolpack Inn, Doctor Bridge and Beatrix Potter's Penny Hill Farm. The scenery of this part of Eskdale is very fine; in view are Scafell and Scafell Pike, Esk Pike and Bowfell, whilst close at hand Harter Fell dominates the south side of the valley.

Doctor Bridge is a substantial former packhorse bridge, widened in 1734 by the then resident of Penny Hill Farm so that he could cross with his pony and trap. As no attempt was made to match the curve of the existing arch, the widening is very obvious. The bridge was on the

The Tale of Mrs. Tittlemouse

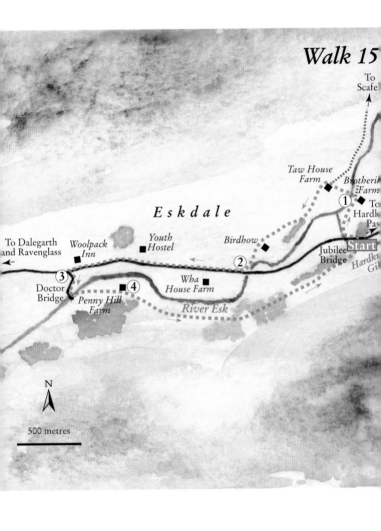

Walk 15

To
Scafe

Taw House
Farm

Brotheri
Farm

① To
Hardk
Pas

E s k d a l e

Birdhow

② Jubilee
Bridge

Start

Hardk
Gi

To Dalegarth
and Ravenglass

Woolpack
Inn

Youth
Hostel

③

Doctor
Bridge

④

Wha
House Farm

Penny Hill
Farm

River Esk

N

500 metres

shortest route for the packhorse traders carrying wool between Whitehaven and Kendal; the nearby Woolpack Inn was a favoured stopping place.

A mile or so from the route of the walk is the Dalegarth terminus of the Ravenglass and Eskdale Railway, a wonderful visitor attraction, with steam-hauled trains throughout an extended season. The station has visitor facilities, including catering.

At nearby Boot is a restored water-powered corn mill.

High beside the Hardknott Pass road to the Duddon Valley stands the superbly sited Roman Hardknott Fort, dominating the upper reaches of the valley.

REFRESHMENTS

Woolpack Inn. Additionally, Brook House and the station at Dalegarth are both less than two kilometres from the route.

CAR PARKING

Roadside spaces for about eight cars at the foot of the Hardknott Pass, grid reference 213012. There are other roadside areas a comparatively short distance down the valley road.

MAP

Ordnance Survey Explorer OL6, The English Lakes, south-western area, 1:25,000.

THE WALK

Start Start down the road. Turn right by the telephone box along the access roadway to Brotherikeld Farm; there is a 'public footpath' sign. Cross a stream; at the approach to the farm there is a National Trust sign 'footpath to Upper Eskdale, avoiding the farm yard'.

(1) Turn left here, cross a sleeper bridge, pass a waymark and another National Trust sign, cross another stream and pass a 'Taw House and Scafell' sign. Turn left to cross a high footbridge over the River Esk. Go over a stile and walk along the edge of a field, directly towards Taw House Farm. Go through a kissing gate into the farmyard, bearing left to follow the farm access drive for a little more than one kilometre, passing the isolated house, Birdhow. Harter Fell is the prominent mountain across the valley.

(2) Join the valley road, keeping right. On the far side is Wha House Farm, with holiday accommodation. Except at really busy periods such as Bank Holidays, the road provides an acceptable walking route. Pass the fine youth hostel before reaching the Woolpack Inn.[1]

ABOVE AND OPPOSITE
Woolpack Inn, Eskdale

1. The Eskdale Showground, where Beatrix competed successfully with her Herdwick sheep, is close to the inn. It was at Eskdale Show that Beatrix first met the celebrated artists Delmar Banner and Josefina de Vasconcellos.

2. Long before the time of Beatrix Potter, this farm was an inn, well-placed on the packhorse route along the valley bottom. After her success with the farms at Sawrey, Beatrix took the opportunity to purchase Penny Hill, although it was far removed from her other property holdings. In common with those others, it passed to the National Trust after her death in 1943.

(3) In less than 200m turn left along a surfaced cul-de-sac roadway, signposted to Penny Hill Farm. Descend to the river, soon reaching Doctor Bridge. Cross the bridge, then fork left towards Penny Hill Farm.[2] Although the old bridleway goes through the farm, the National Trust has arranged a white-waymarked diversionary route for walkers. It is easy to follow, to the right of the buildings, through several gates, rejoining the old route just beyond the farm.

④ Continue along the clear track, through the occasional gate and crossing the occasional small stream, keeping roughly the same height above the valley bottom. In the early part of the route, Harter Fell is ahead. Scafell and the other mighty peaks are all in view. After crossing a more substantial stream, rise to a signposted junction in a short distance.

Go straight ahead, now along a public footpath as the bridleway turns left to Wha House. The next stream, Dodknott Gill, is crossed on a footbridge, followed by a gate as the

path enters sparse woodland. There are more kissing gates and yet another stream; this section of the path is flanked by extensive bracken and the views up the valley are at their best. Join a more major track just before a kissing gate, then pass through another kissing gate in 20m before descending to Hardknott Gill. Cross the gill on the bridge and rise to return to the parking area.

Doctor Bridge, Eskdale

FURTHER READING

As would be expected, very many books and booklets concerning Beatrix Potter, her life and her diverse and outstanding achievements have been written since her death in 1943. Almost all of these books are interesting and entertaining; some have thrown light on previously lesser known aspects of her life.

As a very short and, inevitably, subjective short list, the following are suggested:

1. *The Tale of Beatrix Potter*, Margaret Lane. The first biography.
2. *The Journal of Beatrix Potter, 1881–1897.* Beatrix Potter's own diary, written in a unique code. Transcribed by Leslie Linder.
3. *Beatrix Potter, Artist, Storyteller and Countrywoman*, Judy Taylor.
4. *Beatrix Potter's Art*, Anne Stephenson Hobbs.
5. *Beatrix Potter, The Artist and her World*, Judy Taylor, Joyce Irene Whalley, Anne Stephenson Hobbs, Elizabeth Battrick.
6. *A Victorian Naturalist*, E. Jay, Mary Noble;, Anne Stephenson Hobbs.
7. *Beatrix Potter, The Unknown Years*, Elizabeth Battrick.

Last, but by no means least, the twenty three tales and some other works such as nursery rhymes, written by Beatrix herself. Over the years these have been published in several different formats, including an excellent composite volume of the *Tales*. As individual books the original format remains supreme.

WEBSITES

National Trust:
www.nationaltrust.org.uk

The Armitt:
www.armitt.com

The World of Beatrix Potter:
www.hop-skip-jump.com

The Beatrix Potter Society:
www.beatrixpottersociety.org.uk

Frederick Warne:
www.peterrabbit.com

ACKNOWLEDGEMENTS

Our thanks to:
1. Most of all to Beatrix Potter herself, for the remarkable little books which have delighted and influenced generations of young

and not so young children, for her artwork and for her Journal and her numerous letters, so many of which have survived, illuminating aspects of her life and character. Of at least equal importance, countless residents of and visitors to the Lake District continue to benefit from her foresight in purchasing farms and land, in forestalling inappropriate development and in managing these properties in the traditional manner before bequeathing them to the National Trust. Her legacy is truly breathtaking.

2. To the many experts who have written, spoken publicly and prepared comprehensive exhibitions since her death. Their work has been much appreciated and enjoyed over the years by the present authors and by countless others. Space permits mention of only a very small number: Margaret Lane, Leslie Linder, Judy Taylor, Anne Hobbs, Irene Whalley and Elizabeth Battrick have all contributed a great deal to our understanding of Beatrix Potter.

3. To the various organisations such as the National Trust and the Armitt Trust at Ambleside, who have not only cherished so much of what Beatrix Potter left to posterity, but have made much of that legacy available for public enjoyment. In particular, the National Trust properties at Hill Top Farm and at the Beatrix Potter Gallery in Hawkshead are indispensable to any appreciation of the writer/artist and her work.

4. The Beatrix Potter Society. Founded by enthusiasts in 1980, the Society exists to promote the study and appreciation of the life and works of Beatrix Potter. The Society is a registered charity, with membership worldwide. The activities include biennial Study Conferences in the Lake District and Scotland, regular talks and meetings, usually held in London, and visits to places with a Beatrix Potter connection. The Society publishes a quarterly news-letter, the proceedings of the Study Conferences and other works of original research.

5. The World of Beatrix Potter, Crag Brow, Bowness, a remarkable visitor attraction, where the combination of audio-visual display and wonder-fully realised tableaux of the Potter animal characters has great appeal to many adults in addition to the obvious interest for children.

INDEX

Italics denote illustrations

ILLUSTRATION CREDITS

Cover Pigling Bland & Alexander at the crossroads, National Trust (*The Tale of Pigling Bland*). Copyright © Frederick Warne & Co., 1913, 2002. Jemima Puddle-Duck and the foxy gentleman, National Trust (*The Tale of Jemima Puddle-Duck*). Copyright © Frederick Warne & Co., 1908, 2002. Lucie on the path above Little-Town, National Trust (*The Tale of Mrs Tiggy-Winkle*). Copyright © Frederick Warne & Co., 1905, 2002. **p21** Kep Talks to the hound puppies, National Trust (*The Tale of Jemima Puddle-Duck*). Copyright © Frederick Warne & Co., 1908, 2002. **p29** Jeremy Fisher lands a stickleback, National Trust (*The Tale of Mr. Jeremy Fisher*). Copyright © Frederick Warne & Co., 1906, 2002. **p39** The cook pays the carrier, National Trust (*The Tale of Johnny Town-Mouse*). Copyright © Frederick Warne & Co., 1918, 2002. **p51** The farmer's wife feeds the hens, National Trust (*The Tale of Jemima Puddle-Duck*). Copyright © Frederick Warne & Co., 1903, 2002. **p59** Mrs. Tabitha Twitchit brushes Mittens, National Trust (*The Tale of Tom Kitten*). Copyright © Frederick Warne & Co., 1907, 2002. **p69** Hunca Munca carving ham, National Trust (*The Tale of Two Bad Mice*). Copyright © Frederick Warne & Co., 1904, 2002. **p77** Peter Rabbit and Benjamin Bunny amongst the rocks, National Trust, (*The Tale of Mr. Tod*). Copyright © Frederick Warne & Co., 1912, 2002. **p87** The flopsy bunnies at the open window, British Museum (*The Tale of the Flopsy Bunnies*). Copyright © Frederick Warne & Co., 1909, 2002. **p97** Peter Rabbit eating radishes, Warne archive (*The Tale of Peter Rabbit*). Copyright © Frederick Warne & Co., 1902, 2002. **p103** Pigwig dances for Pigling Bland, National Trust (*The Tale of Pigling Bland*). Copyright © Frederick Warne & Co., 1913, 2002. **p113** Benjamin Bunny and Peter Rabbit looking at footprints, National Trust (*The Tale of Benjamin Bunny*). Copyright © Frederick Warne & Co., 1904, 2002. **p123** Timmy and Goody Tiptoes under an umbrella, National Trust (*The Tale of Timmy Tiptoes*). Copyright © Frederick Warne & Co., 1911, 2002. **p137** 'Squirrels at the edge of lake, making rafts' National Trust (*The Tale of Squirrel Nutkin*). Copyright © Frederick Warne & Co., 1903, 2002. **p151** Mrs. Tiggy-Winkle starching dicky fronts, National Trust (*The Tale of Mrs. Tiggy-Winkle*). Copyright © Frederick Warne & Co., 1905, 2002. **p163** Mrs. Tittlemouse serves cherry stones, National Trust (*The Tale of Mrs. Tittlemouse*) Copyright © Frederick Warne & Co., 1910, 2002.